IMPROVING ASSESSMENT PRACTICE

A REFERENCE GUIDE FOR NVQ ASSESSORS

By Siobhan Maclean

Improving Assessment Practice:
A Reference Guide for NVQ Assessors

By Siobhan Maclean

Images by Kate Durrant

First Edition 2004 ISBN: 1-903575-25-7
Second Edition 2005 ISBN: 1-903575-27-3
Third Edition 2006 ISBN: 1-903575-36-2

A catalogue record for this book will be available from the British Library

©Kirwin Maclean Associates
47 Albion Street
Rugeley
Staffs

ISBN: 1-903575-36-2

Printed in Great Britain by:
Kirwin Maclean Associates Ltd, Rugeley, Staffordshire

CONTENTS

4

INTRODUCTION

This book is written for NVQ assessors. It will be most helpful to new assessors who are working on the new Assessor Qualification. It will also be helpful for anyone who is involved in the assessment of other's performance.

Unit A1 (Assess Candidates Using a Range of Methods) was developed by the Employment National Training Organisation. It replaces the previous D32/D33 units for NVQ assessors. This book is closely linked to the new unit and will help candidates to develop their knowledge and understanding and build their portfolio.

SECTION 1: AN INTRODUCTION TO COMPETENCE BASED ASSESSMENT

As an NVQ assessor you will be responsible for assessing the competence of candidates. This process is known as competence based assessment.

This section introduces NVQs and some of the basic principles of competence based assessment. You might already have a very good understanding of NVQs, in which case you could just skip this section, unless you want to refresh your knowledge.

AN INTRODUCTION TO NVQs

NVQ stands for National Vocational Qualification. As the name implies it is a nationally recognised qualification. In Scotland the qualification is called an SVQ (Scottish Vocational Qualification) so you may see NVQs referred to as S/NVQs. To avoid confusion, some people have dropped the S/N altogether and you may therefore see NVQs referred to as VQs.

The introduction of NVQs was recommended by the Review of Vocational Qualifications Working Group in 1986. NVQs have since been regularly reviewed and refined. NVQs are widespread across practically all work settings. They are not unique to the care sector. In fact there are over 750 NVQs in different areas. Whatever the area covered by the NVQ, whether it be manufacturing, engineering or care, NVQs have a similar structure and share the same basic principles.

NVQs are based on National Occupational Standards (often referred to as NOS) and are very different from traditional qualifications in many ways. For example:

- There are no formal examinations
- NVQs can be gained in a variety of different ways
- They take account of previous experience
- They allow the individual to work and achieve at their own pace
- Assessment is undertaken in the workplace
- Each unit is a separate achievement and can be separately certificated
- National Standards mean that NVQs are transferable to different workplaces

NVQs are set at five levels of competence which are as follows:

Level 1

Competence which involves the application of knowledge and skills in the performance of a range of varied work activities, most of which are likely to be routine or predictable. Level 1 indicates work that is highly supervised and requires very little or no individual decision making, for this reason there is no level 1 in social care.

Level 2

Competence which involves the application of knowledge and skills in a significant range of varied work activities, performed in a variety of contexts. Some of the activities are complex or non-routine, and there is some individual responsibility and autonomy. Collaboration with others, perhaps through membership of a work group or team, may often be a requirement.

Level 3

Competence which involves the application of knowledge and skills in a broad range of varied work activities performed in a variety of contexts, most of which are complex and non-routine. There is considerable responsibility and autonomy, and control or guidance of others is often required.

Level 4

Competence which involves the application of knowledge and skills in a broad range of complex, technical or professional work activities performed in a wide range of contexts and with a substantial degree of personal responsibility and autonomy. Responsibility for the work of others and the allocation of resources is often present.

Level 5

Competence which involves the application of skills and a significant range of fundamental principles across a wide and often unpredictable variety of contexts. Very substantial personal autonomy and often significant responsibility for the work of others and for the allocation of substantial resources feature strongly, as do personal accountabilities for analysis and diagnosis, design, planning, execution and evaluation.

NVQs in Health and Social Care

A revised set of NVQs in health and social care were implemented early in 2005. The current NVQs in health and social care are:

NVQ L2 Health and Social Care

NVQ L3 Health and Social Care *(Children and Young People)*
NVQ L3 Health and Social Care *(Adults)*

NVQ L4 Health and Social Care *(Children and Young People)*
NVQ L4 Health and Social Care *(Adults)*

NVQ L4 Registered Managers Award *(Adults)*
NVQ L4 Award for Managers in Residential Child Care

The Structure of NVQs

I find the easiest way to think about the structure of NVQs is to visualise an NVQ in the form of a family tree, as follows:

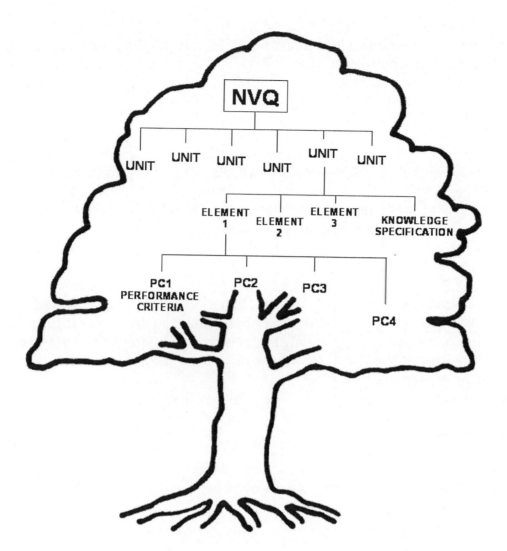

Units

To achieve an NVQ, candidates need to complete a number of individual units. Each unit basically represents an area of work. Some units are compulsory (referred to as core units) whilst others are optional (ie. they can be selected from a list of choices).

The documentation for each NVQ details how many units need to be completed and how units are grouped, which units can be combined etc.

The front sheet of each unit gives a broad description of the work covered in the unit. Clarification is also provided, in each unit, about the language used, any specific requirements etc.

Each unit also provides guidance on the assessment methods to be used (ie. what evidence should be provided). The evidence requirements are clearly detailed and must be followed as the unit is evidenced.

Elements

Each unit is broken down into a number of elements. Each element describes an aspect of work covered by the unit.

For example, if we look at Unit HSC32 which is a level 3 core unit, we can see that it is broken down into three elements, as follows:

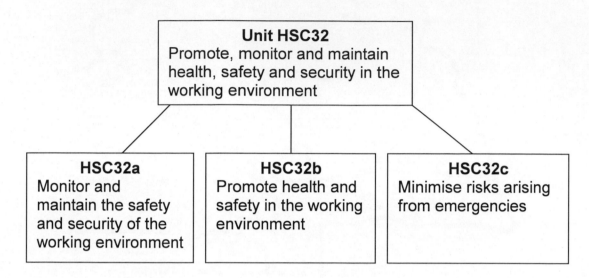

Performance Criteria

Each element is further broken down into performance criteria (often referred to as PC). Each performance criteria basically describes a small piece of work.

Scope

Some performance criteria are broken down further detailing "scope". Scope really explains the areas which may be relevant to particular work roles or working environments. Candidates only need to provide evidence of the scope which is related to their work area. Explanation of what the scope may include is always provided at the beginning of the unit.

Knowledge Specifications

Towards the end of each unit a list of knowledge appears. This details what a candidate needs to understand in order to carry out the work detailed in the unit.

UNDERSTANDING NVQs

1

Look at an NVQ unit and make sure you can find your way around it by answering the following questions:

- What is the title of the unit?

- How many elements are there?

- How many performance criteria are there in the first element?

- How many separate pieces of knowledge are referred to on the knowledge specification?

- What are the evidence requirements for the unit?

Developing Your Knowledge of NVQs

When you first start working with NVQs they can seem very confusing. Your knowledge will develop quickly as you work through units with a candidate. The process of assessment planning with a candidate will enable you to think through what each unit refers to. Attending meetings with other assessors will also help you to develop your understanding. Remember, too, that you will be working on an NVQ unit yourself (Unit A1) and this process will help you to understand the structure and practice of NVQs. Use every opportunity you can to develop your understanding of NVQs.

WHO DOES WHAT IN NVQs?

For many people it feels that just three people are involved in NVQs:

- The candidate
- Their assessor
- The internal verifier

However, you can look wider than this and see that in addition to these three individuals, there are a number of organisations involved in NVQs. The following diagram represents this:

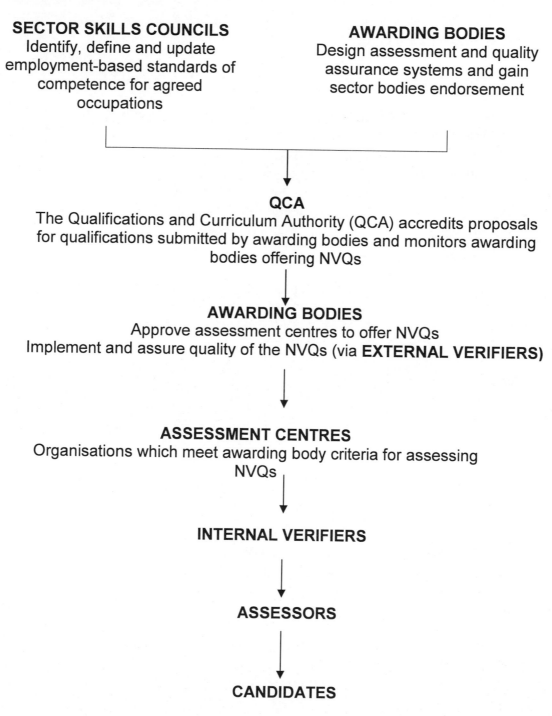

SECTOR SKILLS COUNCILS
Identify, define and update employment-based standards of competence for agreed occupations

AWARDING BODIES
Design assessment and quality assurance systems and gain sector bodies endorsement

QCA
The Qualifications and Curriculum Authority (QCA) accredits proposals for qualifications submitted by awarding bodies and monitors awarding bodies offering NVQs

AWARDING BODIES
Approve assessment centres to offer NVQs
Implement and assure quality of the NVQs (via **EXTERNAL VERIFIERS)**

ASSESSMENT CENTRES
Organisations which meet awarding body criteria for assessing NVQs

INTERNAL VERIFIERS

ASSESSORS

CANDIDATES

Having looked through the diagram you will (hopefully) realise that arguably the most important people have not been mentioned. Of course, service users will be involved extensively in the NVQ process, since it is the candidate's work with service users, which will be assessed. In addition, the purpose of NVQs is to improve practice and ultimately, therefore, the delivery of care and support to service users.

With this overview of who is involved in NVQs, you will be aware that a number of individuals and organisations are involved in the delivery of NVQs. The roles of the four main people involved are covered below:

The Candidate

The candidate's role includes:

- Identifying prior achievement and sources of evidence of that achievement
- Negotiating an agreed assessment plan and any additional development requirements
- Negotiating learning opportunities
- Identifying opportunities for assessment with their assessor
- Collecting evidence and matching this to the standards
- Identifying what is valid and sufficient evidence
- Reviewing own progress with assessor(s) and acting on identified points for development

All candidates should take ownership of the process of evidence collection and actively seek assessment opportunities. Candidates should claim competence by presenting the accumulated evidence to be judged by their assessor.

The Assessor

The assessor's role includes:

- Interpreting the standards
- Carrying out candidate induction and initial assessment ensuring candidates are aware of their own responsibility in the assessment process
- Assessing prior achievement
- Identifying opportunities for candidates to collect evidence and demonstrate competence
- Negotiating individual action plans with candidates
- Identifying valid and sufficient evidence and sources of evidence for the standards
- Judging the candidate's evidence against the criteria over a period of time using a range of assessment methods
- Making objective assessment decisions and giving constructive feedback to candidates

- Identifying gaps in achievement
- Ensuring fair assessment and equality of opportunity for all candidates within the assessment process
- Maintaining records of candidate's progress and achievement
- Reviewing on-going progress and achievements with candidates
- Meeting regularly with other assessors, internal verifier(s) and Centre Co-ordinator (if appropriate), for quality assurance purposes.

The Internal Verifier

The internal verifier's role includes:

- Co-ordinating the provision of a specific qualification (or recognised group of qualifications) within an Assessment Centre
- Ensuring the Centre's quality assurance mechanisms are operating effectively for specific qualification(s) by carrying out a process of internal verification
- Liaising with the allocated external verifier
- Providing support and advice to assessors
- Ensuring that assessors are applying the national standards by sampling assessments and internally verifying assessment decisions, providing prompt feedback to assessors
- Monitoring the Centre's equal opportunities practice with regard to open access to assessment and relating to the Centre's own published equal opportunities policy
- Ensuring that the recording of achievement is carried out accurately
- Completing and signing the Certification Record Forms prior to submission to the awarding body for certification
- Ensuring the on-going training, development and up-dating of the NVQ team
- Ensuring that action points agreed with the external verifier are implemented effectively

It is expected that meetings between the internal verifier and the team of assessors will take place on a regular basis in order to review the assessment process and ensure that all assessors are applying the national standards by sampling assessments and internally verifying assessment decisions. This means that meetings will normally need to occur monthly or bi-monthly according to the level of assessment activity within the Centre.

The External Verifier

The external verifier is appointed by the awarding body and plays a crucial role in the quality assurance system. His/her role is to ensure that the Assessment Centre's quality assurance systems are operating to maintain the national standards by:

- Providing information, advisory and support services to Centres
- Verifying assessment practice and Centre procedures

- Maintaining records of visits and providing feedback to the awarding body
- Disseminating good practice
- Ensuring that the policy of equal opportunities and open access is adhered to

Continued approval as a Centre will be dependent on the receipt by the awarding body of positive external verifier visit reports.

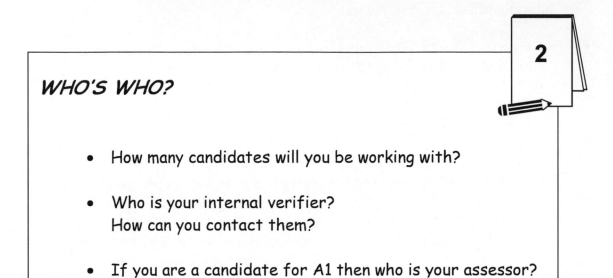

WHO'S WHO?

2

- How many candidates will you be working with?

- Who is your internal verifier?
  How can you contact them?

- If you are a candidate for A1 then who is your assessor?

COMPETENCE BASED ASSESSMENT

As we have said NVQs involve competence based assessment. The principles of competence based assessment, whatever the qualification, are the same.

It is important to be clear about the meaning of competence based assessment before working through this book, and the best place to start is with your own definitions. Exercise 3 helps you to explore these.

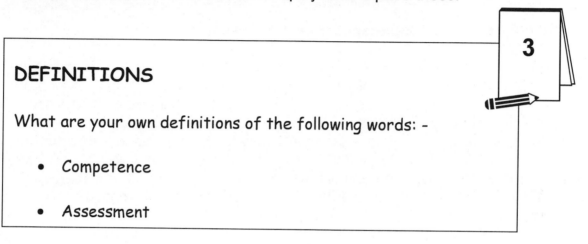

DEFINITIONS

What are your own definitions of the following words: -

- Competence

- Assessment

The following definitions are drawn from a range of sources - considering these, alongside your personal definitions, may assist you in clarifying some of the key terms used throughout this package.

Competence

"Competence is the ability to perform the activities within an occupation or function to the standards expected in employment."

(RSA 1998)

"Competence is the ability to perform the work to a set standard. It is a holistic concept that embraces skills, knowledge and understanding, attitudes and capacity. The emphasis is on application to work – not knowledge or skills for their own sake."

(Rowanhill 2005)

Assessment

"Assessment is the process of interpreting evidence of candidate performance."

(Holloway et al 1995)

"Within a competence based system, assessment is the generation and collection of evidence of performance which can be matched to specified (and explicit) standards which reflect expectations of performance in the workplace."

(Fletcher 1992)

"Assessment is the process o documenting, often in measurable terms, knowledge, skills, attitudes and beliefs. Assessment is often used in an educational context, but applies to many other areas as well."

(Wikipedia 2005)

The Purpose of Competence Based Assessment

In the past qualifications were seen as something people went "off to college" to do. However over recent years there has been a clear recognition of the fact that college based learning needs to be applied and tested in practice. The idea of competence based learning is to enable a candidate to demonstrate what they have learnt and how they apply this to their practice.

Competence based programmes may or may not include a component of college based learning. The aspect which sets competence based programmes apart from traditional training is that they always include an element of competence based assessment. This may be in a candidate's usual workplace or in a practical placement setting.

Competence based assessment is often criticised, perhaps because it takes up more time in the workplace than traditional college based learning. However, it is important to remember that good quality competence based assessment has numerous strengths. Exploring the purpose of competence based programmes helps to clarify the strengths of this form of learning and assessment over traditional models. There are many advantages for individual candidates and the employing agency.

Competence based assessment is designed to:

- Provide the candidate with ongoing feedback on their performance in general, their specific strengths and their areas for development

- Acknowledge the good work done by the candidate and give them the confidence to stretch and explore their skills further

- Identify the areas in which the candidate needs to improve to reach a satisfactory standard

- Identify any areas where a candidate needs specific help, guidance and support

- Monitor levels of performance in relation to the agency's standards and requirements

- Establish a mutual agreement between the assessor and candidate about levels of performance

- Establish the level of competence achieved by the candidate and provide nationally recognised certification of this, where relevant.

(adapted from I.L.P.S. 1993)

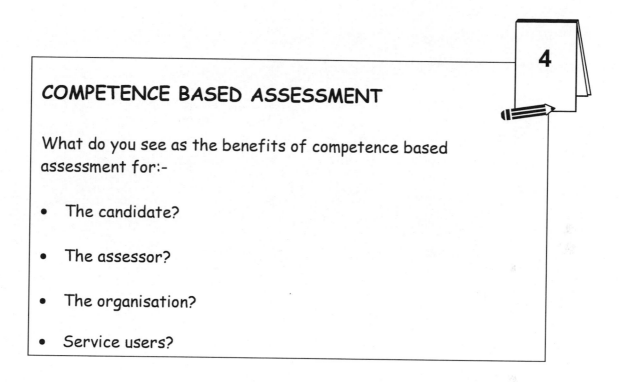

COMPETENCE BASED ASSESSMENT

What do you see as the benefits of competence based assessment for:-

- The candidate?

- The assessor?

- The organisation?

- Service users?

THE ASSESSMENT PROCESS

Any competence based assessment involves four distinct stages:-

- Planning
- Collecting evidence
- Judging evidence
- Providing feedback

Whilst this can be seen in the following diagram, it is important to remember that these stages do not always occur in a neat sequence. It is quite common for assessors and candidates to be working on all four stages of the process simultaneously on different parts of the standards being assessed. Therefore a number of the following assessment cycles may be going on at any one time.

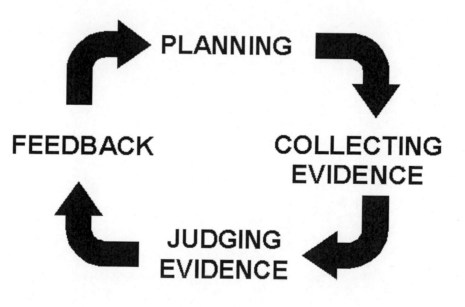

As a qualification for assessors, unit A1 reflects the sequence of the assessment process. Unit A1 is broken down into the following four elements:

A1.1   Develop plans with candidate for assessing competence
A1.2   Judge evidence against criteria to make assessment decisions
A1.3   Provide feedback and support to candidates on assessment decisions
A1.4   Contribute to the internal quality assurance process

The first three elements reflect the process of assessment. You will notice that the only stage of the process which isn't referred to is the collection of evidence. This is because the collection of evidence is the responsibility of the candidate.

In order to provide a structured and informative book for assessors the next three sections of this handbook cover the assessment process, linking into the elements of A1.

SECTION 2:   ASSESSMENT PLANNING

The first (and perhaps most vital stage) of assessment practice is planning the assessment with the candidate. This section covers the key issues to be considered when planning assessments.

Links to A1.1

Develop plans for assessing competence with candidates

EFFECTIVE ASSESSMENT PLANNING

If assessment is to be fair and reliable the candidate must be clear about what is being assessed and how it will be assessed. Clear negotiation and a written agreement are vital.

In planning an assessment the following areas should be negotiated:-

- Which parts of the standards are to be worked on?
- Who will be involved?
- What evidence will be available?
- What evidence is required?
- Dates and times of assessment meetings
- What assessment methods will be used?
- What will be the arrangements for the direct observation of practice?
- What will be the arrangements for feedback?
- Who is responsible for recording the evidence?
- How will evidence for the value base be incorporated?
- Are there any specific assessment requirements? If so, how will they be addressed?
- How will confidentiality and other ethical issues be addressed?
- When will the plan be reviewed?
- How will any difficulties or disputes be handled?

Where problems arise in assessment, these can usually be traced back to problems in the planning stages. Thoughtful planning is essential to effective assessment practice.

The Importance of Assessment Plans

All of the awarding bodies stress the importance of assessment plans in supporting candidates and ensuring they succeed. External verifiers refer to assessment plans to evaluate how effective Assessment Centres are.

The assessment plan is therefore a vital part of assessment documentation.

Benefits of Assessment Plans

Assessment plans ensure that the process of assessment is clear to all involved. This is often referred to as transparency in assessment. In particular, assessment plans:

- Involve the candidate in the assessment process from the outset, encouraging an ownership of the process
- Ensure that assessments are candidate led
- Clarify and formalise the process of assessment for both the candidate and assessor

- Assist in record keeping and tracking planned performance
- Clarify roles, responsibilities and expectations (this is particularly important where others are to be involved in the assessment process)

Being Smart with Assessment Planning

Assessment plans should be made up of:

Specific
Measurable
Achievable
Realistic
Targets

Recording Assessment Plans

Whilst we have said that assessment plans should be SMART, the actual way in which you record assessment plans is not vital. Some Assessment Centres provide specific assessment plan formats, whilst others suggest assessors and candidates use the assessment planning column in each unit assessment record.

There are a variety of ways of recording an assessment plan and as an assessor you will probably find that you use different methods with different candidates. Probably the most important aspect of an assessment plan is that the candidate understands what is expected of them and is motivated to move on. Therefore, because candidates will have very different styles you will probably find that your assessment plans look quite different.

Even with the same candidate you might find that assessment plans for different units are recorded differently. Because:

- A candidate may be more experienced in some tasks than others and therefore more confident about some units than others
- As a candidate progresses through their NVQ they may be more proactive in the planning of further units
- Some units link very closely and so you may plan for a group of units together.

Essentially, you need to negotiate with the candidate to find a method of recording your plans that are accessible to both of you and can be understood by a third party (for example, the internal verifier).

Reviewing Assessment Plans

As can be seen from page 23 assessment planning is the first step in the process of assessment. However, an assessment plan is never complete until the process of assessment is complete. It should be kept under constant review and renegotiated whenever necessary. Assessment plans may need to be modified/changed for a number of reasons. They should be a working document and reflect changes and candidate progress.

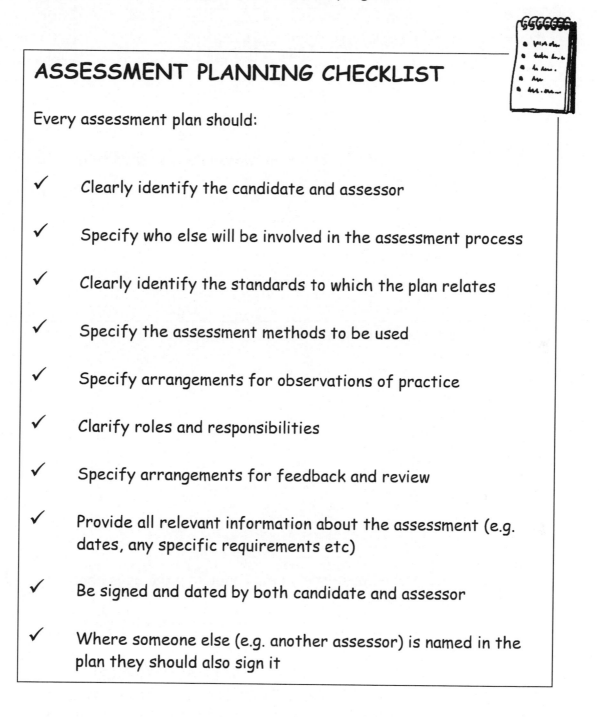

ASSESSMENT PLANNING CHECKLIST

Every assessment plan should:

✓ Clearly identify the candidate and assessor

✓ Specify who else will be involved in the assessment process

✓ Clearly identify the standards to which the plan relates

✓ Specify the assessment methods to be used

✓ Specify arrangements for observations of practice

✓ Clarify roles and responsibilities

✓ Specify arrangements for feedback and review

✓ Provide all relevant information about the assessment (e.g. dates, any specific requirements etc)

✓ Be signed and dated by both candidate and assessor

✓ Where someone else (e.g. another assessor) is named in the plan they should also sign it

Don't forget!

ASSESSMENT PLANS NEED TO BE KEPT UNDER REVIEW. THEY SHOULD BE UPDATED WHENEVER NECESSARY.

EXPLORING ASSESSMENT PLANS

Look back over some of the assessment plans you have completed, either as a candidate or as an assessor.

- Does the assessment plan cover all the points referred to in the assessment checklist on page 29?

- In what ways could you improve the plan?

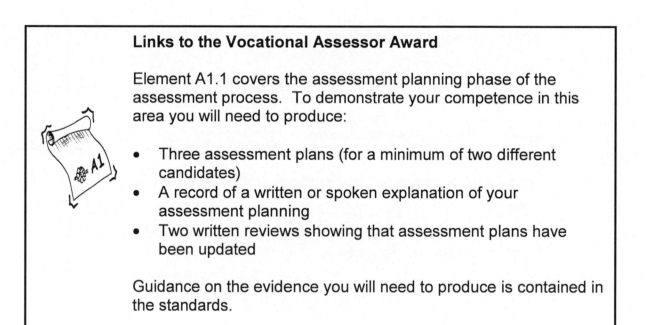

Links to the Vocational Assessor Award

Element A1.1 covers the assessment planning phase of the assessment process. To demonstrate your competence in this area you will need to produce:

- Three assessment plans (for a minimum of two different candidates)
- A record of a written or spoken explanation of your assessment planning
- Two written reviews showing that assessment plans have been updated

Guidance on the evidence you will need to produce is contained in the standards.

Don't forget!

KEEP COPIES OF ALL YOUR ASSESSMENT PLANS AND REVIEWS SO THAT YOU CAN GATHER THE EVDIENCE YOU NEED FOR YOUR OWN PORTFOLIO

SECTION 3: MAKING ASSESSMENT DECISIONS

The next stages of the assessment process are collecting evidence and judging evidence. It is the candidate's responsibility to provide evidence to the assessor. The nature and type of evidence required therefore needs to be clearly identified in the assessment plan.

As a general rule:

a) The candidate is responsible for collecting and providing evidence with support and suggestions from the assessor
b) The assessor is responsible for judging the evidence.

This section goes on to consider collecting evidence and judging evidence as distinct phases of the assessment process.

Links to A1.2

Judge evidence against criteria to make assessment decisions

32

COLLECTING EVIDENCE

Many candidates find identifying evidence to match specific criteria difficult, at least initially. They know they have done/regularly do what is required but find providing evidence of this difficult (i.e. they know they have done something but can't _prove_ that they have done it).

The triangulation model works well in terms of identifying evidence (particularly in terms of performance evidence). The model is based on the following triangle of assessment methods, or evidence sources.

Observation of Practice
(including direct observation and less commonly video and audio evidence)

Testimonial Evidence
(feedback – preferably written - can be provided by a variety of people e.g. line manager, colleague, service user, co-worker etc)

Product Evidence
(including recording, letters, memos etc).

Where a candidate can think of work they do that demonstrates the criteria, each corner of the triangle should be considered in terms of identifying relevant evidence e.g:-

- Observation of practice – can I arrange an observation of this work?
- Testimonial evidence – who has seen me do this and how can I get feedback from them?
- Product evidence – what record do I have of the work?

Observation is always the strongest source of evidence as it is easy to apply the VACS rules of evidence (see page 47). However, it may not always be possible or appropriate to observe certain areas of practice. The two other corners of the triangle should then be considered. Where the candidate and assessor are not able to identify evidence using the triangulation model it is likely that the best source of evidence would be a candidate's reflective account of the work they have identified as meeting the standards.

The full range of assessment methods (or sources of evidence) are outlined in this section. It is always useful in exploring any area of practice to start with your own experiences. Exercise 6 therefore helps you to consider your own experiences and perspectives

EXPLORING ASSESSMENT EXPERIENCES   6

Please write what you do now, not what you think you should be doing.

• If you were asked to provide evidence that you are competent in your job, what evidence could you produce?

• If you have given any qualification as examples of evidence, how do these qualifications actually relate to what you do in your job and how well you do it?

• What methods have been used to assess you in the past?

• Which of these methods do you feel were most effective and why?

The choice of assessment methods must be negotiated between the candidate and assessor as part of the assessment plan. Decisions about the selection of methods will be influenced by the following:-

• Are we looking for evidence of the candidate's knowledge or performance?
• What are the assessment requirements of the criteria?
• What is the context of the assessment? (For example are there any operational constraints?)

Cost effectiveness and time constraints will also influence the choice of assessment methods. In working through these questions candidates and assessors should be able to identify the most appropriate methods of assessment.

Direct and Indirect Methods of Assessment

Essentially, all methods of assessment can be categorised into either direct or indirect methods of assessment.

Direct

This is sometimes referred to as primary evidence. Direct methods of assessment refer to evidence provided directly by the candidate, for example:

- Product evidence
- Observations of practice
- Results of questioning

Primary evidence is the most straightforward form of evidence for an assessor to use in terms of matching to standards because it is the most straight forward to judge. However, it can also be the most time consuming in terms of the time required to observe or question practice.

Indirect

This is sometimes referred to as secondary evidence. Indirect methods of assessment are methods which provide evidence *about* the candidate for example:-

- Testimonial evidence
- Training records
- Certificates

It is worth considering what you are looking for when choosing whether to use a direct or indirect method of assessment. On the whole if you are looking for performance evidence you will want to use direct methods of assessment.

GIVING A TAP DANCER A WRITTEN TEST WON'T TELL THE ASSESSOR MUCH ABOUT THE DANCER'S SKILLS

UNDERSTANDING ASSESSMENT METHODS

DIRECT OBSERVATION

Direct observation always includes at least three parties: the candidate, the assessor, and the service user(s) or fellow professional(s) with whom the candidate is engaged. Each party has a different role to play in the observation. It is important to remember that where service users are involved their needs necessarily take priority over those of the candidate and assessor.

The Potential of Direct Observation

Direct observation of practice has many benefits. In fact, it can be so helpful to all involved that where direct observations of practice have been carried out, candidates and assessors continue to arrange occasional observations even after any assessment has concluded.

For candidates, direct observation provides opportunities to:-

- Reflect upon their practice
- Benefit from the assessor's perspective on the candidate's work
- Demonstrate competence and receive confirmation of their abilities
- Identify areas of difficulty and obtain advice and support

For assessors, direct observation provides opportunities to:-

- Understand the candidate's current abilities
- Identify areas for further work and provide relevant learning opportunities
- Obtain evidence for assessment

For service users, direct observation has the potential to:-

- Act as a safeguard, through the scrutiny of a candidate's work by a more experienced practitioner (the assessor)
- Improve the service received
- Create an opportunity to evaluate the service received and give feedback

Practical Issues

Observations need to be carefully planned with candidates as part of the assessment planning process. It is important to remember that candidates who are not used to being observed may be particularly anxious about being observed and this needs to be clearly discussed. Where a candidate is very clear about what you are looking for in an observation their anxiety will be better managed.

WE ALL DO STRANGE THINGS WHEN WE ARE INTIMIDATED!!!!

Remember, the service user/carer must always give permission for the observation. Where they are used to your presence this may be easier to negotiate. However, as a general rule the candidate is responsible for getting permission from the service user and explaining your role as an observer. Service users who have good understanding of the observation process are less likely to be distracted by the assessors presence.

It is important to remember though, that in any direct observation of practice, the presence of the observer (the assessor) is likely to have an impact on the situation.

A useful model for the direct observation of practice has been developed for social work students by the University of York (University of York 2000). This model involves using areas for discussion between the candidate and observer following the observation. The broad 'headings' to be used in this discussion are:

- Surprises
- Satisfactions
- Dissatisfactions
- Learning

Both the candidate and assessor can share their thoughts using these broad areas. I find this can provide a useful structure to discussions following the observation. For example, when discussing surprises I can gauge whether there were any changes to the situation based on my presence. When discussing satisfaction and dissatisfaction I also get an idea about whether what I have observed is at the same standard as the candidate's usual practice etc.

Remember, it is very important to record your observation against the standards, as soon as possible. Providing this to the candidate can form part of your feedback and review session.

Direct observation evidence can be supplemented by video or audio evidence of practice.

Video Evidence

Whilst video evidence can be used, it is fraught with difficulties such as:

- obtaining the necessary equipment

- ethical issues about videoing service users and associated confidentiality concerns
- candidates can find videoing uncomfortable

Since there are so many inherent difficulties I would recommended that video evidence is used only in exceptional circumstances when discussed and agreed within the Assessment Centre.

Audio Evidence

Again audio evidence of practice has ethical dilemmas in terms of service user involvement, and needs to be carefully considered before being used.

FEEDBACK FROM OTHERS

Also referred to as third party feedback, testimonial evidence or witness testimony, this can be a strong source of evidence.

It is always important to negotiate the form feedback should take, with candidates. On the whole written feedback is preferable and some Assessment Centres provide a pro-forma for this.

Feedback can be sought from a range of people:-

Feedback from Colleagues

Often, colleagues are in a strong position to provide feedback on a candidate's practice. They may, for example, have worked alongside a candidate on an aspect of work relating to the standards.

Feedback from Service Users

There can be obvious problems inherent in service user feedback. For example, the power dynamics of the service user/candidate relationship can have a significant impact on the feedback. However, it is important to involve service users in the assessment process and this is now more widely recognised.

The form that service user feedback takes and the method for collecting it will vary, so it is important to negotiate with the candidate as early as possible about gaining service user feedback. It may be most appropriate to seek feedback from service users following direct observations.

Of course, there may be situations where getting service users feedback will be more difficult – for example where service users do not communicate verbally. Those who know the service user (eg: an advocate) may be able to advise or provide feedback. Carers (eg: service users family and friends) may also be able to give feedback in this situation. Creativity is important in gaining service user feedback.

<u>Feedback from Other Professionals</u>

Other professionals can provide a good source of evidence for some criteria. However, it is important to remember that other professionals may not have a full understanding of the role of a social care worker so the feedback may need to be weighed against this.

<u>Feedback from Line Manager</u>

In many situations the role of assessor is taken on by the candidate's line manager. Where this is not the case it is vital that the assessor gets formal feedback across a range of criteria from the candidate's line manager.

General Guidance

Feedback is only helpful where it is clear and relevant to the criteria being assessed. It may be very pleasant for a candidate to receive written feedback saying the candidate "is a very good worker", but what exactly does that mean? Whoever seeks the feedback (usually the candidate) needs to be very clear about what they are looking for, so that the testimonial evidence relates directly to the criteria being assessed.

PRODUCT EVIDENCE

Product evidence basically refers to anything that has been produced by the candidate as part of their work.

Candidates will routinely complete case recording, they may also write letters and reports. All of these can be strong sources of evidence. The assessor should have routine access to agency documentation completed by the candidate and this evidence should be discussed as part of the assessment process.

Some criteria will mean that product evidence must be viewed by the assessor. For example, if the criteria relates to the way a candidate records, then the assessor must obviously see some of this recording. In using such product evidence it is vital to ensure that confidentiality is maintained (see section 7).

In some situations the assessor may use the way the candidate organises the setting as evidence of competence and this could be considered a work product (e.g. the way a candidate prepares a bathroom to assist a service user to have a bath).

OTHER EVIDENCE

Whilst the triangulation model basically covers evidence which is naturally occurring, other evidence produced or generated specifically for the assessment process can be useful. This may include the following:

Simulation/Role Play

Simulation or role play can be useful to assess candidates where their routine work practice would not include them demonstrating the criteria. Simulations may take place in the candidate's actual work setting or away from it. A simulation may be more stressful to candidates than doing the real thing, so it is important to prepare and debrief everyone concerned.

Certain types of competence that are regarded as critical to the occupational role of workers with service users may be difficult, if not impossible, to observe for practical or ethical reasons or because the competence is only rarely demanded. For example, response to an emergency situation, or handling disclosure of abuse. In such cases simulation exercises are an acceptable next best alternative. For example, carrying out a fire drill would be an obvious alternative to burning an establishment down in order to assess the candidate's competence in dealing with a fire emergency!

However, role plays and simulations should only be used sparingly since assessment should, as far as possible, be about a candidate's work in actual work situations.

Reflective Accounts

Candidates may write reflective accounts about critical incidents in their work practice. These can be strong sources of evidence. However, since they rely on self reporting it is important to balance these with other evidence for verification purposes. It is not unknown for candidates to produce fantastic, thoughtful, reflective accounts which bear no resemblance to the work undertaken!

Questioning

Questioning can take many forms ranging from oral questions (e.g. discussions), to a candidate completing written questions. Because of the unpredictability and nature of much of the work in the care sector you might find yourself asking a lot of 'what if' and 'why' questions in order to supplement performance evidence and meet range requirements. It is worth spending time really getting to know the standards and their requirements, setting down your expectations of candidates and subjecting these to critical scrutiny to make sure you are not expecting too much or too little or simply expecting the candidates to think as you do rather than meet the requirements.

Whatever form the questions take it is important that the answers given by the candidate are recorded in some way if they are to be used as a reliable source of evidence. However be aware that:-

"if the unit of competence does not demand writing skills you should not ask for written answers to questions unless the candidate is happy with this approach".

(CCETSW 1992)

One of the basic principles of NVQs is that they do not involve and "examination". Where candidates are asked to complete written question papers, this undermines the aim of NVQs to be accessible and work related. Audiotaping or minuting discussions relating to work activities is therefore preferable to written questioning.

Projects/Assignments/Case Studies

These can provide good sources of evidence. However, it is important to remember that whilst written work may provide good quality evidence of a candidate's knowledge and understanding it may tell you more about their ability to write coherently than about their work practice.

It is also important to remember that requesting written evidence of this kind when it is not a specific programme requirement may disadvantage some candidates with specific needs.

Evidence from Past Achievement

This is sometimes referred to as APEL (Accreditation of Prior Experience and Learning), APL (Accreditation of Prior Learning) or APA (Accreditation of Prior Achievement).

Evidence drawn from previous experience can be problematic for a number of reasons:-

- You need to be clear that it relates to the standards
- You need to be clear that the candidate is still competent in this area
- It may be more difficult to check the authenticity of evidence provided

As a general rule, where candidates have relevant prior experience this should be discussed as part of the assessment plan. Where current evidence is available this should then be utilised. If it is difficult to obtain current evidence, ask for advice on the use of past evidence from the Assessment Centre.

Assessment Method	Provides Evidence of	Strengths		Weaknesses	Notes
Observation of Practice	Performance (and sometimes knowledge)	✓ provides quality evidence ✓ should be undertaken as part of line manager's usual responsibility		✗ opportunity for direct observation of some areas may be limited ✗ can create 'false' working practice	• need for clear planning
Testimonial Evidence	Performance (and sometimes knowledge)	✓ involves range of relevant people in assessment process ✓ promotes reflective practice		✗ people providing testimonials may not understand the criteria ✗ can be power issues/difficult dynamics	• need for clear explanation to those giving feedback
Product Evidence	Both performance and knowledge	✓ naturally occurring			• confidentiality requirements must be clear
Reflective Accounts,	Both performance and knowledge	✓ can help candidates to illustrate the actual application of knowledge to practice ✓ can be helpful where triangulation model (i.e.: above 3 methods) do not identify evidence.		✗ candidates may 'struggle' with written work ✗ may provide evidence more of candidates ability to write fluently	• be clear about the task
Case studies, projects, assignments etc	Knowledge (and possibly performance)	✓ can be well structured to elicit key areas of knowledge and understanding ✓ can set projects etc to cover a full range of criteria		✗ removed from real working conditions ✗ candidates may 'struggle' with written work ✗ may provide evidence more of candidates ability to write fluently	• be clear about the task
Questioning	Knowledge (can also cover range)	✓ provides good supplementary evidence ✓ valuable tool for collecting knowledge evidence and clarifying other evidence		✗ assessors can answer their own questions!	• assessor needs good questioning technique • answers should be recorded fully

43

ASSESSMENT METHODS CHECKLIST

When negotiating assessment methods with candidates always ensure that a range of methods have been used. You can draw from:-

✓ Direct Observation

✓ Testimonial Evidence

✓ Product Evidence

✓ Case Studies

✓ Simulation/Role Play

✓ Projects/Assignments

✓ Questioning

✓ Evidence from Prior Achievements

EXPLORING ASSESSMENT METHODS

Given below is a list of possible assessment methods. Note which of these you would use. Indicate what you would be assessing using that method. If you do not/would not use a particular method write your reason for not using it.

- **DIRECT OBSERVATION**

I would use this to assess:

I would not use this method when:

- **SIMULATION**

I would use this to assess:

I would not use this method when:

- **PRODUCT EVIDENCE**

I would use this to assess:

I would not use this method when:

- **PROJECTS AND ASSIGNMENTS**

I would use this to assess:

I would not use this method when:

- **TESTIMONIAL EVIDENCE**

I would use this to assess:

I would not use this method when:

JUDGING EVIDENCE

So far in this section we have covered the assessment methods which may be utilised to gather evidence of competence. Once a candidate has gathered the evidence agreed in the assessment plan they will present it to their assessor. The assessor is responsible for judging the evidence presented. Various issues need to be considered when judging evidence. One method of judging evidence which is often used and referred to (probably because it's easy to remember!) is judging evidence against the "VACS" criteria.

Validity – the key question assessors must ask when considering each piece of evidence presented by the candidate is "what does this evidence tell me?" It may tell you something about the standard or it may tell you about some other work activity. Check that the evidence actually matches the criteria it is presented for. On occasions candidates present evidence of an excellent piece of work, but it relates to a different performance criteria, or even a different unit. In this case your feedback to the candidate should include guidance about where this evidence could be used instead.

Authenticity – if competence is to be attributed to an individual on the basis of evidence presented, there must be no doubt that it relates to that individual's own work. Where evidence relates to joint working, this is particularly important and the assessor will need to check out with the other person/people involved which part of the work is the candidate's own.

Consistency – competence must be demonstrated on more than one occasion and over a period of time. As a general rule evidence should 'date' across the period of assessment, so that not all the evidence is drawn from one day, one piece of work etc. The C can also stand for currency – is the evidence presented current?

Sufficiency – sufficient evidence needs to be collected to demonstrate beyond all reasonable doubt that the candidate has performed to the standards of the performance criteria. This can create difficulties for assessors in terms of "how much is enough?" Assessors should use standardisation meetings and feedback from the internal verifier to help them answer this question. It is important to remember that a candidate does not need to present a 'new' piece of evidence for each competence requirement. In fact one piece of evidence can provide evidence against a whole host of criteria. If candidates had to produce new evidence for each performance criteria candidates and assessors would be pushing portfolios round in wheelbarrows!

Safe, Fair, Valid and Reliable?

Unit A1 requires you to make safe, fair, valid and reliable decisions against standards. This is essentially at the heart of making assessment decisions.

Following the guidelines in this book will ensure that all of your assessment decisions are safe, fair, valid and reliable. For example working systematically within the assessment process (as outlined in Section 1) will ensure that your assessment practice is 'safe'. Applying values to your assessment will ensure that your decisions are 'fair' (as covered in Section 7). Using a range of relevant assessment methods and applying the VACS rules of evidence will ensure your decisions are 'valid' and 'reliable' (see earlier in this Section).

MAKING ASSESSMENT DECISIONS

In your view what are some of the factors you should consider in deciding whether evidence is:

- Safe
- Fair
- Valid
- Reliable

If you apply the VACS criteria, you are checking that the evidence is what?

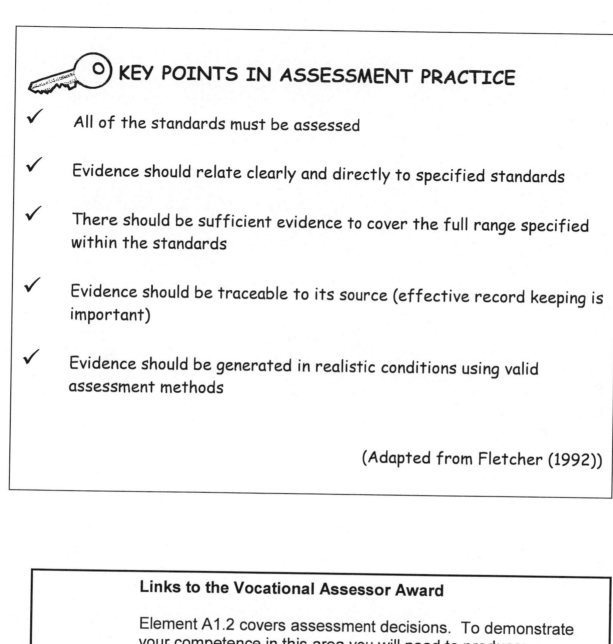

KEY POINTS IN ASSESSMENT PRACTICE

✓ All of the standards must be assessed

✓ Evidence should relate clearly and directly to specified standards

✓ There should be sufficient evidence to cover the full range specified within the standards

✓ Evidence should be traceable to its source (effective record keeping is important)

✓ Evidence should be generated in realistic conditions using valid assessment methods

(Adapted from Fletcher (1992))

Links to the Vocational Assessor Award

Element A1.2 covers assessment decisions. To demonstrate your competence in this area you will need to produce:

• Three assessment decision records (for a minimum of two different candidates)
• A record of a professional discussion (with your assessor) showing how you have met the requirements stipulated in the standards

You need to read the standards for guidance on this evidence.

SECTION 4:   PROVIDING FEEDBACK ON ASSESSMENT DECISIONS

You need to give candidates ongoing feedback throughout the assessment process. This section covers the provision of feedback to candidates.

Links to A1.3

Provide feedback and support to candidates on assessment decisions.

THE IMPORTANCE OF FEEDBACK

Based on the evidence provided you need to make a decision about whether or not a candidate is competent. This decision must be recorded in the required format. However, this is by no means the end of the process. The assessor needs to communicate the decision to the candidate and provide them with feedback. The key to good assessment practice is the provision of good quality feedback in good time.

Feedback can be either positive (that is, re-enforcing good practice) or negative (that is, feedback on poor performance). Both positive and negative feedback can be constructive. Where feedback is constructive it will enable the receiver to develop their practice. Where feedback is missing or destructive the receiver will not be able to develop effectively.

Feedback is a vital part of the assessment cycle in that feedback where a candidate is deemed 'not yet competent' will enable the candidate and the assessor to review and adapt the assessment plan. Where a candidate is judged to be competent feedback is still a vital part of the process and will enable the candidate to plan for their future development beyond the achievement of the qualification in question. It is important that candidates never feel that once they have completed a qualification they have no more to do. The achievement of any qualification is always part of a continuum of professional development.

During our lives, we often receive feedback on our performance from line managers, peers, family etc. Sometimes the feedback we receive makes us feel encouraged and motivated. At other times, feedback can be damaging and destructive. Exercise 9 helps you to reflect on this.

FEEDBACK EXPERIENCES 9

- Think of an example of a situation where feedback on your performance made you feel encouraged and motivated.

- Think of an example of a situation where feedback on your performance discouraged you and made you demotivated.

- Consider the factors, which contributed to each. What was it about the feedback you received that made you feel encouraged or discouraged? NB: Remember to focus on the actual feedback rather than what it was about.

Constructive Feedback

Constructive feedback provides information about the candidate's performance against the specified standards in such a way that the candidate maintains a positive attitude towards themselves, their work and the qualification. It encourages candidates to commit themselves to a personal action plan to move towards the agreed standards. Constructive feedback is intrinsically linked to the process of learning. When you provide effective feedback you are helping the recipient to learn. The following guidelines will help you to think through what makes feedback constructive and therefore effective.

GUIDELINES FOR GIVING CONSTRUCTIVE FEEDBACK

In working as an assessor, you will often hear the term "constructive feedback", but what makes feedback "constructive"? Exercise 9 will have given you some ideas based on your own experiences of receiving feedback. The following guidelines will also help make clear what constructive feedback means in practice.

Positive

Feedback should always start and finish with a positive. This is often referred to as the positive sandwich. The content of the sandwich gives the candidate something to work on, whilst the 'bread' is the positive aspects. In this way the candidate's esteem and motivation will be built on.

Specific

Deal clearly with particular instances and behaviour rather than making vague or sweeping statements. For example "*when asking about mobility, you moved too quickly through the questions rather than allowing the person to fully answer*". Rather than "*your listening skills were rubbish*".

Descriptive

Use descriptive rather than evaluative terms. For example, "my perception was that when you repeated the same question several times the person became confused", rather than "your questioning technique was confusing".

Actionable

Direct feedback towards behaviour that the candidate can do something about. For example, "if you slowed down your delivery, it would probably be easier for the person to follow what you were saying", rather than "your accent is hard to understand."

Prioritised

Concentrate on the two or three key areas for improvement, preferably including those where the candidate can see a quick return. Break down a major problem into smaller, step-by-step goals. (This is the 'content' of the positive sandwich).

Offer alternatives

Offer suggestions to what could have been done differently. Turn the negative into a positive. For example, "when you remained seated at the start it seemed unwelcoming. Shaking her hand and smiling would have helped set up a better rapport".

Well-timed

The most useful feedback is given when the candidate is receptive to it and it is sufficiently close to the event to be fresh in their mind.

Facilitative

Rather than prescribing behaviour, feedback should help the candidate question their behaviour and make them aware of where they are going wrong. For example, *"How might that have been interpreted by the service user?"*

Clear

Avoid jargon wherever possible and ensure that your communication is clear. Always check feedback to ensure that it is understood by the recipient.

It's Not What You Say It's the Way that You Say it

No doubt, you will have heard this said a number of times. As a competent worker you will be aware of the importance of effective communication. However, it's worth re-visiting this concept in terms of feedback.

Research has shown that what you say contributes only a small part of the message heard by the listener. For example, Mehrabian and Ferris (1967) found that:

- What you say (ie: the words used) accounts for 7% of the message received.

- How you say it (ie: the tone of voice, the emphasis given to words and the volume and pace of what you say) accounts for 38% of the message received.
- How you look when you say it (ie: body language – posture, facial expression, eye contact etc) accounts for 55% of the message received.

Don't forget all your basic skills when providing feedback to candidates!

Feedback can be given badly and whilst the scenario in exercise 10 seems extreme, it happens.

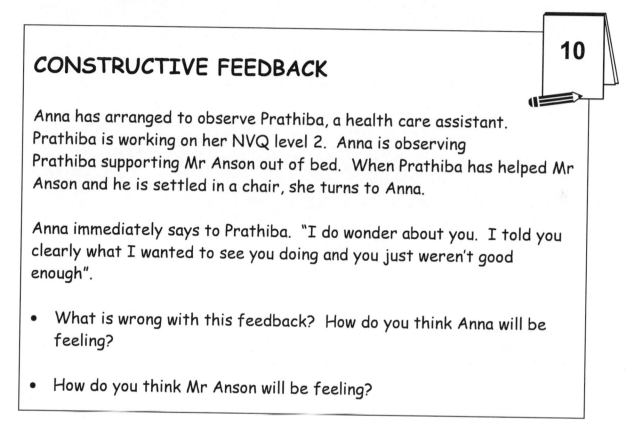

CONSTRUCTIVE FEEDBACK

10

Anna has arranged to observe Prathiba, a health care assistant. Prathiba is working on her NVQ level 2. Anna is observing Prathiba supporting Mr Anson out of bed. When Prathiba has helped Mr Anson and he is settled in a chair, she turns to Anna.

Anna immediately says to Prathiba. "I do wonder about you. I told you clearly what I wanted to see you doing and you just weren't good enough".

- What is wrong with this feedback? How do you think Anna will be feeling?

- How do you think Mr Anson will be feeling?

USING THE ASSESSMENT PROCESS POSITIVELY

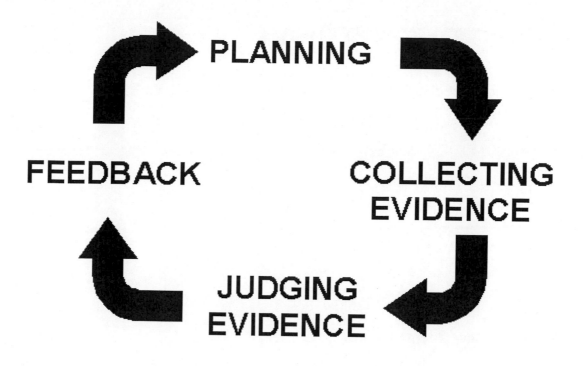

PLANNING

FEEDBACK

COLLECTING EVIDENCE

JUDGING EVIDENCE

If you keep the four phases of the assessment process in mind, you can clearly see that if your feedback to the candidate concludes by stating that they have not yet demonstrated competence then the next stage is to amend the assessment plan.

Where this is occurring regularly you will be alerted to the fact that there are some difficulties in the assessment. It is important to make others aware at this point. Discuss the situation with the internal verifier, they should be able to offer advice and support.

Every Assessment Centre has procedures for dealing with situations where the candidate is not providing sufficient evidence of competence. It is vital that you are familiar with these so that you know what to do in this situation.

You must make contact with others as early as you are aware that there are problems, or the potential that the candidate will not demonstrate competence. This will help you to evaluate the situation and make plans to address it.

Don't forget!

CHECK YOUR ASSESSMENT CENTRE GUIDELINES AND MAKE SURE YOU KNOW WHAT TO DO IN THIS SITUATION.

11

REFLECTING ON FEEDBACK

Following a feedback session with a candidate think about the following questions:

- What were my objectives?

- What was the outcome?

- What went well? Why?

- What didn't go so well? Why?

- What have I learnt?

- Might I handle this differently next time? How?

Don't forget!

THE BEST WAY TO DEVELOP YOUR FEEDBACK SKILLS IS TO GET FEEDBACK ON YOUR FEEDBACK!

WHEN FEEDBACK IS DIFFICULT

Feedback on assessment decisions can be difficult for a range of reasons. Fears about the responses of candidates, particularly to negative feedback, can inhibit assessors in giving accurate feedback. However, it is vital to give honest feedback to candidates, throughout the assessment process, as has been covered.

What do I do if the candidate disagrees with the feedback?

This can be problematic as you won't be able to move on through the process of assessment, until there is some level of agreement between you.

If the candidate disagrees with the facts you are basing your feedback on then:

- Give detailed examples.
- Check the areas of disagreement eg: "Do you think 'it' didn't take place or are you disagreeing about details of 'it'?"
- Clarify the candidates version of events and have an open mind.

If the candidate disagrees that a problem exists ("everyone makes mistakes") then explain the consequences of the action. Point out that making mistakes does not constitute competence, so you will need to see positive evidence for the standard in question.

What do I do if they start crying?

If you ensure that your feedback follows the guidelines given, this is unlikely. However, if a candidate does cry when you are giving them feedback, then:

- Be empathic eg: "I understand you will be shocked if no one has talked to you about this before."
- Give permission for the person to cry (it can relieve stress).
- Talk about why the candidate is finding the feedback upsetting.
- Try not to put off the session. It may be tempting to do so, but if you do, you will be leaving the candidate with the distress. Try to move on, instead, to finding solutions which will end the session on a positive note.

What do I do if they get angry?

A natural defence mechanism when a person feels under pressure is anger. If a candidate becomes angry, then:

- Be empathic eg: "I understand why you feel shocked/angry...."

- Find something to say that agrees with the candidate eg: "I know that you are working hard on this area in difficult circumstances."
- Don't be put off giving the feedback. The person may be using anger as an avoidance technique.

DEALING WITH RESPONSES

12

Mike has arranged a feedback session with one of his candidates Louise. Mike is concerned that Louise hasn't fully understood the criteria. She has provided some good evidence, but it doesn't really relate to the criteria being assessed.

Mike is very thoughtful about his feedback. He informs Louise that his decision about the unit is that she still needs to provide some more evidence. Louise starts to cry, Mike is very uncomfortable and is unsure what to do.

- What should Mike do?

Links to the Vocational Assessor Award

Element A1.3 covers the provision of feedback to candidates. To demonstrate your competence in this area, you will need to produce:

- At least one report on an observation carried out by your assessor. This must be supported by written evidence of feedback to two other candidates.
- A record of a professional discussion (with your assessor) showing how you have met the requirements stipulated in the standards.

You need to read the standards for guidance on this evidence.

SECTION 5:   PROBLEMS IN ASSESSMENT PRACTICE

This package has given you good practice guidelines on assessment practice, but so far it has focussed on assessment in positive situations (ie: where candidates have produced sufficient evidence of their competence). However, there can be situations where a candidate fails to produce evidence of their competence despite the opportunities they have had, or where things "go wrong" in other ways.

This section covers some of the problems which may occur in assessment practice.

WHEN THINGS "GO WRONG"

There can be a range of situations where the candidate does not produce evidence of their performance which meets the assessment standards, or where things "go wrong" in other ways.

It is common in such situations for the assessor to question themselves. It is always helpful to begin with an examination of the assessment process and your role in this, but beware of "blaming yourself". This said, you may find it useful to work through the following questions. These are designed to help you identify the root of the "problem" and then to try and identify a strategy to deal with the situation, perhaps designing a new, more effective, assessment plan.

Power and Powerlessness

Have you addressed this with the candidate in a way that would enable them to demonstrate competence? *See Section 7.*

Assessment Plans

Is the assessment plan clear about what is expected? Was this negotiated clearly with the candidate? Has it been kept under review and updated as necessary? *See Section 2.*

The Assessment Process

Have you worked through the assessment process in a systematic way, i.e. planning, gathering evidence, judging evidence, giving feedback? *See Page 23.*

Feedback

Have you given clear constructive feedback to the candidate throughout the assessment? *See Section 4.*

Specific Needs

Have you clearly considered any specific assessment requirements and addressed these in the assessment? *See Section 7.*

Partnership

Have you worked in a way which is candidate led, giving the candidate support where required?

Opportunities

Has the candidate benefited from sufficient opportunities to demonstrate competence?

Assessment Methods

Have you used a sufficient range of assessment methods to enable the candidate to demonstrate competence? *See Section 3.*

The Context of Assessment

Do you and the candidate fully understand the assessment criteria? Have you sought advice and support from relevant people? (e.g. Internal verifier)

Don't forget!

REFLECTING ON YOUR PRACTICE IN SITUATIONS WHERE CANDIDATES ARE NOT YET COMPETENT CAN HELP TO IMPROVE YOUR ASSESSMENT SKILLS. HOWEVER, IT IS VITAL NOT TO BLAME YOURSELF – THIS PROCESS IS CANDIDATE LED AND IF THE CANDIDATE HAS NOT DEMONSTRATED COMPETENCE THIS IS VERY UNLIKELY TO BE THE ASSESSOR'S "FAULT".

WHAT'S GOING "WRONG"?

13

- James has dyslexia. He has informed Anita, his assessor, about this. When considering knowledge requirements Anita always sets written questions and asks for answers in writing. This saves her time. James has not provided evidence for any full unit.
  What could be "going wrong"?

- Brian has assessed Jane's portfolio and signed it off as competent. After the internal verifier has sampled it, the unit is returned. She says that she has noticed that the candidate's reflective accounts seem to be written in various different handwriting.
  What could have "gone wrong"?

COMMON SOURCES OF ERROR IN THE ASSESSMENT OF COMPETENCE

So far this handbook has considered the process of assessment by looking at the four key stages. Whilst assessment appears to work in a neat cycle errors can occur at any stage of the process. The most common errors are as follows.

Halo/Horns Effect

The 'Halo' effect involves assessors inferring good practice on the part of a candidate on the basis of previous good performance by that candidate, without him/her actually being required to demonstrate the performance to the current standard. The previous performance may not have been associated with the criteria now being assessed.

The 'Horns' effect is similar to the halo effect, only the opposite. On the basis of previous 'not-competent' performance by the candidate an expectation exists that future performances will also be 'not-competent'. Instead of waiting for the performance, the assessor infers (probably wrongly) that these future performances will be 'not-competent'.

Stereotyping

Stereotyping is always dangerous and directly contravenes the professional value base. In relation to assessment, stereotyping can occur in terms of assuming a certain level of competence (or lack of competence) based on an apparent characteristic of a candidate. An example would be an expectation that a young person might not be expected to be competent in assisting a bereaved person, on the grounds that they don't have sufficient 'experience of life'.

It is not only the assumption itself which is dangerous, but also the way in which it might lead an assessor to look for certain pieces of evidence.

Remember whenever we assume it makes an ASS out of U & ME

First Impressions

This involves an assessor 'taking a liking' to a candidate (or the opposite) and on the basis of this first or early contact viewing the candidate's performance more or less favourably than should be the case.

If you imagine a candidate who is warm and welcoming when you first meet him/her you can also imagine how difficult it is to be objective, especially if being objective means perhaps jeopardising that warmth.

Similar to Me

This involves judging a candidate favourably because they carry out a piece of work like we would or have values which are just like ours. 'Ours' may be the wrong way or not the required way!! It is also important to remember that there are often many ways of carrying out a task. Just because a candidate does something in a different way doesn't mean they are not competent.

Contrast Effects

This arises when one candidate's performance is compared to that of another candidate by an assessor. The inferior performance may then be deemed not competent, no matter how it stands compared to the performance criteria and evidence requirements. Candidates must be assessed against criteria, not against each other.

Crediting 'Nice' People

Crediting those who in everyday life strike us as pleasant/nice people who we warm to and want to spend time with. It is common to make the jump from liking them not just on the basis of a casual contact but perhaps on the basis of more established contact to inadvertently 'conspiring' with them to help them through the assessment.

The opposite can happen just as easily!

Giving More Weight to the Negatives than the Positives

This occurs where a candidate has performed in a manner contrary to that required by the standard on one occasion – perhaps in very significant area of work. In order to be satisfied that s/he is meeting the criteria and the need for consistency, we then expect many more competent performances or more evidence than is asked for before we agree the competence exists.

Benefit of the Doubt

Where a performance has not conclusively met the performance criteria or fully provided the evidence which is required this error involves giving the candidate the "benefit of the doubt". Agreeing that s/he is competent on the basis of what evidence is provided – insufficient as it is.

If you are not sure that the evidence has been provided don't side with the candidate – err on the side of caution. Be conservative in your judgement – make sure.

Inferring or Generalising

Don't work on the basis that 'because the candidate can do A, s/he can also do B, C and D'. Only generalise when the guidance notes tell you that it is safe to do so. Remember, once again, if you ASSUME you make an ASS out of U and ME.

Experimenter Effect

If you're not normally around the candidate whilst they are working, then your observing him/her will possibly intimidate the candidate – your presence influences the performance. We all do strange things when we are intimidated! This may also have an effect on the way others involved in the observation (eg: service users, colleagues of the candidate) act. This can also affect the candidate's performance. One way to check that the experimenter effect hasn't been an issue is to ask the candidate after an observation "Did anything surprise you?" (See page 38)

Excessive Demands for Evidence

Make sure that the precise evidence, which you are looking for, is neither inadequate nor excessive. Make a judgement on what is the right amount of evidence, in partnership with the candidate based on the assessment documents. Check this out with other assessors at quality meetings etc. Once competence is demonstrated it is wasteful to ask for more demonstrations of the performance, and frustrating to the candidate.

Excessive demands are equally as damaging to assessment as insufficient demands.

Not Understanding the Performance Criteria

Unless you are thoroughly familiar with the standards you will not be able to help candidates to understand what is required of them, nor identify whether the evidence produced matches that which is required.

The best way of coming to an understanding of the standards is by discussing them with colleagues, in support groups, quality panels etc.

The countersigning of assessments, internal verifier sampling of assessment judgements and standardisation meetings are all efforts to reduce the possibilities of error to a minimum. It is important to recognise that such error is inevitable in complex social relationships, such as those which exist where people are being assessed, and to guard against it.

ANY OF THESE ERRORS CAN OCCUR AT ANY STAGE OF THE ASSESSMENT PROCESS

SECTION 6: PLAYING YOUR PART IN QUALITY ASSURANCE

Quality assurance arrangements must be in place in every Assessment Centre. Everyone involved in the Centre has a part to play in these arrangements. This section helps you to develop your understanding of quality assurance in NVQs and your role in this.

Links to A1.4

Contribute to the internal Quality Assurance process

AN INTRODUCTION TO QUALITY ASSURANCE

Quality Assurance is about just what it says – assuring quality. Put another way quality assurance is about maintaining standards.

Effective quality assurance is vital for a range of reasons. In terms of NVQs effective quality assurance allows everyone to have confidence about the qualification. All those candidates who demonstrate competence, and only those who do so will be awarded an NVQ. This means that employers, service users and the public in general can have a confidence about social care.

Quality Assurance in NVQs is largely laid out in the NVQ Code of Practice published by the Qualifications and Curriculum's Authority (QCA). Many of the requirements detailed in this section are taken from this Code. The Code is applicable to the delivery of all NVQs not just those in care. Awarding bodies publish guidance, which add to the code and give specific guidance on qualifications in your area. It is important that you have access to all of the quality assurance requirements, which relate to your assessment practice. Make sure you are familiar with all relevant requirements

In NVQs many people play a role in quality assurance (ie: "checking" the standard of NVQ delivery) as can be seen from the diagram on page 15. Essentially you need to be aware of internal systems of Quality Assurance (ie: quality assurance within your Assessment Centre).

"assessment systems cannot be appreciated from the outside…. The spectator sees very little of the game. To appreciate the strengths and weaknesses of any system, the best observations are made from the middle of the team"

Cotton, J (1999)

Awarding bodies require Assessment Centres to put quality assurance arrangements in place. The required systems include Assessment Centres having "explicit and documented" procedures for internal verification to ensure:

- the accuracy and consistency of assessment decisions between assessors operating within the centre;
- that assessors are consistent in their interpretation and application of the national occupational standards contained within the award.

(Q.C.A. 2001)

Internal verifiers therefore have a key role to play in Quality Assurance. To carry out this function they are responsible for:

- regularly sampling evidence of assessment decisions made by all assessors across all aspects of NVQ assessment in order to monitor, and ensure, consistency in the interpretation and application of standards within the centre. Sampling must include direct observation of assessment practice;
- maintaining up-to-date records of internal verification and sampling activity and ensuring that these are available for the purposes of external verification;
- establishing procedures to develop a common interpretation of the national occupational standards between assessors;
- monitoring and supporting the work of assessors within the centre;
- facilitating appropriate staff development and training for assessors;
- providing feedback to the external verifier on the effectiveness of assessment;
- ensuring that any corrective actions required by the awarding body are implemented within agreed timescales.

(Q.C.A. 2001)

It is vital that in addition to understanding the role of the internal verifier in relation to quality assurance, assessors also understand their distinct responsibilities and how these relate to quality assurance. Working through this book will have clarified your role in working with candidates. This section helps you to relate your responsibilities to Quality Assurance in NVQs.

THE ASSESSOR'S ROLE IN QUALITY ASSURANCE

In order to contribute to internal systems of Quality Assurance, assessors must:

- keep accurate records which are up-to-date
- contribute to standardisation arrangements
- communicate information on assessments through outlined communication channels.

Recording

You must keep your assessment records up-to-date. The records which you keep need to be open to scrutiny. When recording think about the following:

- Can they be understood by a third party?
- Can a candidate's progress be clearly 'tracked' through your recording?

You will get advice from your internal verifier about the records you are expected to complete. Some Assessment Centres require only paper based recording and others expect computer recording. Make sure you know what records you are expected to complete, who needs to see them, and how you keep them.

It is easy to lose sight of the importance of assessment records with the range of competing demands that workers face. However, the importance of these cannot be under estimated. However good you are at assessing, providing feedback etc, your assessment practice will not be effective if you do not keep the necessary records.

Don't forget!

ALL RECORDS SHOULD BE STORED SECURELY ALTHOUGH YOU WILL NEED TO ACCESS THEM REGULARLY TO UPDATE THEM

Standardisation

Every Assessment Centre will have different arrangements for standardisation (that is ensuring that every assessor is using the standards in the same way). Basically, standardisation means that the same candidate offering the same evidence would be assessed similarly by different assessors.

Standardisation arrangements in Assessment Centres will always include internal verifiers sampling (monitoring) assessments. The assessments completed by new assessors will be verified (checked) by internal verifiers more regularly than those of experienced assessors.

Sampling

The sampling strategy which each Assessment Centre develops will vary according to the needs of the Centre. However, it will always be agreed with the external verifier. Sampling will involve the internal verifier reviewing the quality of assessors judgements at both interim and summative stages:

Interim sampling involves the internal verifier "dipping" into the assessment process at different stages. This might involve reviewing assessments before a decision has been made by an assessor.

Summative sampling entails the internal verifier reviewing the quality of assessment decisions by tracking how the assessor has reached that decision.

Other Strategies

Standardisation strategies might also involve the internal verifier calling standardisation meetings with a group of assessors; providing guidance for assessors about elements where inconsistency has been noted. You need to be clear what standardisation strategies your assessment centre has developed and play your part in these to ensure that your assessment decisions are in line with those of other assessors.

14

UNDERSTANDING "SAMPLING"

- What does your Assessment Centre's sampling strategy require internal verifiers to do? For example, how much of your work will they be sampling?

Communication

Effective quality assurance relies upon open channels of communication between everyone involved in the assessment process. You therefore need to make good use of the communication channels established within the Assessment Centre. For example, you need to have regular contact with your internal verifier and keep them informed about the progress of your assessments. If you have any queries or concerns it is vital that you consult the internal verifier as soon as possible. Make sure that all communication is two way, read the information provided to you by the Assessment Centre, attend the meetings you are invited to on a regular basis etc.

Play Your Part

It is vital that assessors are clear about their role and responsibilities both in general and specifically in relation to quality assurance.

QUALITY ASSURANCE IS VITAL.
EVERYONE INVOLVED IN THE ASSESSMENT
CENTRE HAS A ROLE TO PLAY IN THIS.

15

CONTRIBUTING TO QUALITY ASSURANCE

- What do you need to do to contribute to Quality Assurance in your Assessment Centre?

- Why is Quality Assurance important?

Links to the Vocational Assessor Award

Element A1.4 covers your contribution to the internal Quality Assurance process. To demonstrate your competence in this area, you will need to produce:

- Two assessment records (for different candidates) which have been used as part of the internal quality assurance process.
- Written evidence of your review of at least two pieces of evidence each for two candidates. Again, this evidence must have been used as part of the internal Quality Assurance process.
- A written statement from your internal verifier showing that you have contributed to agreed Quality Assurance procedures.

YOUR OWN PROFESSIONAL DEVELOPMENT

An essential aspect of quality assurance is ensuring your own continuing professional development. You should be supported by the internal verifier you work with, to identify your own needs in relation to your continuing professional development. Once you have identified these you need to work out a strategy to meet the learning needs in conjunction with your manager and/or internal verifier.

Everyone's development needs will be different and the best way for people to address these will be different too. However, there are often key issues for all assessors in particular centres at certain times. For example, over the next year or so, most assessors will need to become familiar with the revised NVQs and new National Occupational Standards. Since many assessors will have this need in common briefings should be provided in centres.

The development needs of new assessors will obviously involve the completion of Unit A1 and new assessors should have developed a time plan and strategy for this. However, experienced assessors should also work on developing a continuing professional development plan which identifies and plans for their individual needs.

Ensuring your own continuing professional development is important to ensure the quality of your assessment practice and to demonstrate your own commitment to a learning culture of which NVQ assessment is an integral part.

SECTION 7: VALUES AND ASSESSMENT

The value base of social care is about concepts such as equality and anti-oppressive practice. Just as these concepts have to be put into practice by candidates, then they must be reflected within assessment practice. This section covers issues of values as they relate to assessment practice.

ASSESSMENT VALUES

The General Social Care Council have developed values for work based assessors in social care. The GSCC identify assessors as key individuals enabling staff to carry out their responsibilities as outlined in the Code of Practice. As such work based assessors should apply the following values in their work.

The values for social care work based assessors:

- Identify and question their own values and prejudices, the use of authority and power in the assessment relationship, and recognise and act upon the implications for their assessment practice;

- Update themselves on best practice in assessment and research on adult learning and apply this knowledge in promoting the rights and choices of learners and managing the assessment process;

- Respect and value the uniqueness and diversity of learners and recognise and build on their strengths, and take into account individual learning styles and preferred assessment methods;

- Accept and respect learners' circumstances and understand how these impact on the assessment process;

- Assess in a manner that does not stigmatise or disadvantage individuals and ensures equality of opportunity. Show applied knowledge and understanding of the significance of

  - Poverty
  - Racism
  - Ill health and disability
  - Gender
  - Social class
  - Sexual orientation

in managing the assessment process;

- Recognise and work to prevent unjustifiable discrimination and disadvantage in all aspects of the assessment process, and counter any unjustifiable discrimination in ways that are appropriate to their situation and role; and

- Take responsibility for the quality of their work and ensure that it is monitored and appraised; critically reflect on their own practice and identify development needs in order to improve their own performance, raise standards, and contribute to the learning and development of others.

General Social Care Council (2002)

EQUALITY OF ACCESS TO NVQs

It is vitally important that all candidates have equal access to assessment. At times this will mean operational adaptations may be required e.g. to ensure that night care workers have the same access to assessment as daytime workers. In some situations providing equal access will be about adapting your assessment practice rather than any specific operational issues.

The main starting point is to recognise that all candidates are individuals with diverse backgrounds and situations. In your initial meetings with candidates you need to consider with the candidate whether they have any specific assessment requirements.

Some of the individual situations which have an impact on assessment are outlined in this section. However, it is important to remember that this is not an exhaustive list and there may be other circumstances which create specific requirements in terms of assessment. The key to effective assessment is to ensure that you see every candidate as a unique individual with their own specific needs and requirements.

Candidates with Disabilities

Where a candidate has a disability, you need to negotiate with them as soon as possible, what support they will require and how the assessment methods to be utilised may need to be adapted (e.g. the provision of case studies in large print or braille). Where the candidate will also have taught input at a college, you should liaise with them to ensure that appropriate assessment takes place. The following checklist is helpful in considering effective assessment practice with candidates with disabilities:

✓	Encourage and value disabled candidates
✓	Negotiate with everyone in the work setting to maximise the candidate's opportunities
✓	Ask the candidate what will best help them
✓	Familiarise yourself with the role of the support worker/enabler (if appropriate) and ensure that everyone involved in the assessment understands the role
✓	Ensure that the candidate has access to any necessary technology
✓	Challenge any barrier within yourself or your agency which blocks the candidate's ability to function, participate and develop
X	Don't patronise

(Adapted from Moss, Marsh and Stockman 1997)

Candidates with Literacy Difficulties

Candidates who have dyslexia will almost certainly have difficulties with literacy; since the condition can include:-

"systematic difficulties with spelling; slow reading and comprehension; slow disjointed handwriting; miscopying; inability to present ideas clearly on paper....."

(Moss, Marsh and Stockman 1997)

Other candidates may have problems with literacy. For example, many candidates in social care have been out of education for many years and their literacy skills may not be particularly advanced.

To manage this you need to ensure that you do not request written evidence where this is not required by the standards. Be creative, candidates can audiotape reflective accounts etc.

Where candidates have particular literacy difficulties or a learning difficulty such as dyslexia, additional support may be available. Discuss any concerns with the Assessment Centre as early as possible in the assessment process.

Candidates from Discriminated Against Groups

Research demonstrates that people from discriminated against groups such as black people and people with disabilities are likely to have had negative experiences in education:

"People from discriminated against groups are used to having their knowledge and experience devalued and disbelieved, both individually and communally"

(ILPS 1993)

Candidates from discriminated against groups may therefore have specific requirements in terms of assessment. For example, assessors should take into account the negative previous experiences that the candidate has had in ensuring they create a safe environment for assessment. Assessors should also understand that the fear of prejudice and discrimination may mean that the candidate is not open in their exchanges with the assessor which may inhibit their performance.

Candidates who Lack Confidence

Candidates may lack confidence for a range of reasons. For example, candidates who have not been supported through continual constructive feedback on their work may lack confidence in their work.

Candidates who lack confidence will need encouragement to work in partnership with their assessor. Effective assessment planning will be especially important to ensure that candidates who lack confidence are clear about what exactly they need to do to demonstrate competence. Assessors will also need to provide regular constructive feedback which builds on the candidate's confidence.

As previously stated, this list is not exhaustive. Candidates may have specific assessment needs for a range of other reasons, such as:-

- Negative previous experiences of assessment
- Limited experience
- Working pattern – shift workers etc.

In addition, some candidates may belong to more than one of the groups outlined in this section. For example, candidates with literacy difficulties may also lack confidence (perhaps as a direct result of their literacy difficulties).

The most important thing is to negotiate with candidates on an individual basis about their assessment requirements. Remember that candidates may not always articulate their difficulties due to apprehension or stigma. Be clear that you will not discriminate against candidates on the basis of any specific assessment requirements.

16

ENCOURAGING CANDIDATES WITH SPECIFIC ASSESSMENT REQUIREMENTS

- Can you think of any specific assessment requirements which may be an issue for your candidates?

- How might you encourage candidates with different levels of confidence to take an active part in the assessment process?

ETHICAL ISSUES IN ASSESSMENT

A number of ethical dilemmas can arise during competency based assessment.

Intrusion

One of the most difficult issues is that of intrusion into the privacy of service users and carers. Assessors and candidates should discuss this in detail as part of the planning process. This has been recognised for some time now:

"When negotiating with the candidate the selection of methods for gathering evidence, the assessor must make certain that the methods selected do not intrude on the rights of [service users] and their carers."

(CCETSW 1992)

There may be some situations where, for example, direct observation of practice may be overly intrusive. It must always be remembered that service users consent for observation needs to be obtained and that they have the right to withdraw this consent at any point.

Asking the candidate to explore the issues surrounding service users' and carers' rights and the tensions that arise in terms of the candidate's assessment may be a helpful strategy in terms of this. It aids the assessor in terms of exploring ethics in assessment and will also help the candidate to demonstrate evidence for the value base unit.

Confidentiality

Service users and carers have a right to confidentiality. This can be inadvertently breached in the assessment process. It is vital that candidates and assessors work to ensure that confidentiality is upheld.

Your Assessment Centre will produce guidelines on the methods of anonymising evidence to ensure confidentiality is maintained. Explanations should be given to service users and others involved in the assessment about the methods used to uphold confidentiality. The way a candidate approaches confidentiality in their assessment will provide you with evidence of the candidate's competence in this area.

Candidates also have the right to confidentiality in terms of their assessment. You must store assessment documentation and portfolio's securely. Don't leave them on your desk where they can be seen by others. Again, your Assessment Centre should provide guidelines in relation to confidentiality for candidates.

The Data Protection Act (1998) covers the way in which information should be handled. You will, no doubt, be familiar with this in terms of your work practice but don't forget that it also applies to your assessment practice.

Quality of Service Provided to Service Users

It is vital to remember that the primary focus in all situations must be the quality of the service provided to the service user and not the assessment of the candidate.

Commitment to service quality can be lost where candidates and assessors are overly enthusiastic about the assessment process. It is important that the candidate and assessor always check the service user's willingness with them at all stages of the assessment process.

Remember too, that your role as an assessor is about the safeguarding of standards of practice. Your role is not about "getting the candidate through" rather it's about "is this candidate competent?"

Don't forget!

THE QUALITY OF SERVICE PROVIDED TO SERVICE USERS MUST ALWAYS BE THE MAIN PRIORITY. PRINCIPLES OF SERVICE DELIVERY SUCH AS CONFIDENTIALITY AND DIGNITY MUST BE UPHELD.

POWER AND ASSESSMENT

The process of assessment creates an unequal role relationship – that of assessor and assessed. The assessor occupies an authority role which is intrinsically more powerful. People being assessed may feel resistant to the assessment process. They may also fear or feel hostile towards the assessor. Past experiences influence expectations, and candidates who bring with them painful or unjust experiences of assessment may find the prospect of assessment particularly daunting. Candidates with visible or invisible differences which could make them the target of discrimination may have specific concerns about being assessed fairly. (See pages 81-83).

In order to work effectively with the power differentials inherent in the assessment process it is important to have a clear understanding of the different forms of power within the assessor/candidate relationship:-

- Professional power – the professional opinion of assessors is likely to be given more weight than the opinions of candidates etc.

- Resource power – assessors have power over resources, and can utilise this power to access or withhold learning and assessment opportunities.

- Societal power – assessors could have societal power. Certainly they do in terms of the "assessor/candidate" relationship. There may be additional dynamics such as a male assessor/female candidate, white assessor/black candidate. But we must also remember here that the candidate may have some societal power, for example a female assessor/male candidate.

- The power to determine - this is perhaps the issue which is most acute in the candidates mind. Assessors have the power to make a decision about whether a candidate is competent or not yet competent, and so to "determine" the future of the candidate (as far as the candidate is concerned).

It can be tempting to deny the power imbalance in an assessment situation. However, this makes the issue more difficult to manage. Best practice is to discuss the power issues and negotiate how the impact of these will be managed.

Techniques for Reducing the Effects of the Power Imbalance

- Be clear about the process of assessment – i.e. negotiate during your assessment planning who will do what and when.

- Ensure that the assessment is candidate led. This increases their control over the situation.

- Discuss the power issues rather than denying them.

Empowerment in Assessment

You will be familiar with the principles of empowerment in terms of your work in care. It is also important that you work in an empowering way with candidates.

To be empowered people need to know as much as possible about what is going to happen and why. Thoughtful, thorough assessment planning is therefore vital.

Where candidates have not experienced competence based assessment before they are likely to draw comparisons with their last experience of education. There is a tradition of being passive in education, of the 'learner' feeling unable to ask questions. Good quality assessment practice recognises the possibility of candidates taking on a passive role and attempts to address it by:

- Creating an enabling environment where questions are encouraged
- Promoting partnership
- The provision of accessible and relevant written and verbal information

Complaints and Appeals Procedures

All Assessment Centres should have a clearly written complaints and appeals procedure. Again, issues of power have a direct bearing, for if candidates feel that they will face some form of reprimand for complaining they will be reluctant to do so. Candidates need to be well informed about appeals and complaints procedures and they need to feel confident about using these if they wish to.

Complaints and appeals procedures are not just about addressing particular issues that have arisen. Good procedures are about equality and encouraging candidates to have a say in the operation of the Assessment Centre.

SECTION 8:   PUTTING YOUR OWN PORTFOLIO TOGETHER

So far, we have referred to unit A1 in terms of the links with sections of the book. This section, however, is dedicated to advising candidates for A1 about their own portfolio.

YOUR OWN ASSESSMENT

Just as you are working through the assessment process with your candidate/s you will have an assessor working through the process with you.

You should therefore work in partnership with your assessor to:

Devise an assessment agreement

Use the information provided in Section 2 to ensure that the assessment plan contains all of the information necessary. As you work on the development of this plan you should be able to demonstrate, through discussion with your assessor, how you negotiate assessment plans with candidates. Remember, therefore that this can be a good opportunity for you to demonstrate aspects of A1.1 and the knowledge required (ie: knowledge numbers 5, 19).

Collect evidence/Judge evidence

Remember, that it is your role to gather the evidence required and your assessor's to make a judgement about whether this evidence meets the specified requirements.

The evidence you need to collect for A1 is very clearly specified within the standards. An excellent overview of the evidence needed is provided in the unit overview. In this book, we have also given you information about the evidence you need to produce.

Your assessor will make a judgement about the evidence you provide and will provide you with feedback on this, hence completing the assessment process. You may then need to review your original assessment plan to decide on the next steps.

Evidence Details

Professional Discussion

As part of your assessment you will engage in discussions with your assessor (eg: as described in relation to assessment planning). Under unit A1 these discussions are to be more formalised for evidence purposes.

The purpose of each professional discussion should be agreed in advance (perhaps as part of your assessment planning).

It is preferable for these professional discussions to be held at your workplace, so that you can refer to any documentation etc which you have. Meeting at your own workplace will mean that your assessor can also see how you handle this documentation in terms of confidentiality and security.

During the discussion you can outline aspects of your work and provide explanations of your practice (as specifically required for elements 1, 2 and 3). Your assessor can ask questions and seek clarification on your explanation.

A full record of the meeting is required in your portfolio which could be in the form of a written record, audio tape or video tape. Remember if you are using audio or video evidence in your portfolio it needs to be accompanied by details of where (eg: at what point) the evidence can be found.

I would advise planning at least four separate professional discussions:

- One to cover assessment planning (A1.1)
- One to cover assessment decisions (A1.2)
- One to cover feedback (A1.3)
- One to cover knowledge not addressed by other evidence.

You can plan the discussions using the relevant PC and the evidence guidelines.

Professional discussion is increasingly being used in NVQ portfolios and you may find that you can use a similar method of assessment with your candidates. Remember though to provide them with clear information about what will be covered in each discussion.

Observation

Your assessment practice will be observed at least once (see A1.3 evidence requirements). This observation will be of your providing feedback to a candidate. You will need to seek permission from the candidate for this session to be observed (make clear that the assessor is observing you and not them).

Your assessor will complete a report of the observation, which will be included in your portfolio. A checklist for this report is provided within the standards. Your assessor should also provide you with feedback immediately following the observation.

A great deal of thought has been put into the use of direct observation as an assessment method in A1. As you will have seen in Section 3 direct observation is the strongest source of evidence in any assessment. However, in view of ethical issues, particularly intrusion (see Section 7), thought needs to be given about which part of your practice should be observed. You can imagine a situation where a service user is being supported by a care worker who is being observed by an assessor, whilst an assessor is observing them. The service user probably wouldn't feel too comfortable!

The observation of your practice for A1, should therefore only involve:

- You
- The candidate
- Your assessor

Independent Assessment

To ensure standardisation across A1 and transparent assessment an independent assessor (ie: a qualified assessor who is not your main assessor) must assess a "substantive component" of your evidence. The independent assessor will be someone completely independent from you and will be selected on this basis by the Assessment Centre you are registered with.

The independent assessor will usually be involved in assessing some of the product evidence included in your portfolio. They will not usually be involved in observing your practice or in engaging in professional discussions with you. Although they may want to see the evidence generated from observations and discussions.

Independent assessment is becoming more common in NVQs as the standards are reviewed and revised. The purpose of independent assessment is to provide an additional element of quality control and should be welcomed in terms of quality assurance.

Ask your assessor how an independent assessor will be involved in your assessment, so that the element of independent assessment is clear to all involved. It is most likely that the independent assessor will become involved towards the end of your assessment when your portfolio is beginning to take shape.

Don't forget!

ALL OF THE EVIDENCE YOU PROVIDE DURING YOUR ASSESSMENT MUST COME FROM YOUR ACTUAL WORK WITH CANDIDATES.

DEVELOPING YOUR PORTFOLIO

The evidence which you generate during your assessment will be gathered into a portfolio. You will be familiar with portfolio style assessment from both previous work based qualifications you have completed and from your role with candidates.

The portfolio you need to complete for A1 should be straightforward in that the evidence you need to produce is so clear.

MAKE A JUDGEMENT ON WHAT IS THE RIGHT AMOUNT OF EVIDENCE

You will probably be tempted to put a great deal more in your portfolio. However, if you do put in more evidence than is required you are indicating that you haven't understood the requirements. Keep your portfolio to the evidence required. Portfolios can very easily put on weight (in this I suppose they are very similar to the rest of us!). However, the more you put in, the less structured and focussed your portfolio will be.

All of the evidence included in your portfolio must be drawn from your actual assessment practice. You cannot include any simulated evidence such as evidence generated during training sessions or your responses to the exercises included in this book. You may like to refer to these during your professional discussions (perhaps to demonstrate how your knowledge has developed etc) but this type of evidence should not be included in your portfolio.

You are responsible, with advice and support from your assessor, for developing your portfolio and indexing the evidence in a way which can be clearly understood by a third party (eg: the independent assessor and the internal verifier).

The most important thing in terms of developing your portfolio is to be familiar with the evidence requirements. All too often, candidates for A1 are very familiar with the requirements of the Award which they are assessing but not the requirements of the Award which they are undertaking. Make sure that you are as familiar with the requirements for A1 as you are with the requirements your candidates are working on.

UNDERSTANDING YOUR A1 PORTFOLIO

Make sure you have the A1 requirements with you before working through the following questions.

- What evidence do you need to produce for A1.1?

- What evidence do you need to produce for A1.2?

- What evidence do you need to produce for A1.3?

- What evidence do you need to produce for A1.4?

- How many observation records do you need to include in your portfolio?

- Do you think you will experience any challenges in developing your A1 portfolio? How will you address these challenges?

DEVELOP YOUR PORTFOLIO AS YOUR WORK WITH CANDIDATES AND YOUR OWN ASSESSMENT PROGRESSES. DON'T LEAVE IT ALL UNTIL THE END.

REFERENCES

CCETSW (1992) "National Vocational Qualifications in Care: Notes on Assessment and Guidance" (London) CCETSW.

Clarke, D. (1996) "Mentoring" (Ely) Fenman Ltd.

Fletcher, S. (1992) "Competence Based Assessment Techniques" (London) Kogan Page.

General Social Care Council (2002) "Guidance on the assessment of Practice in the workplace". (London) GSCC

Holloway, A. MacNeill, F., Robertson, C., Smith, J. and Willcocks, G. (1995) "HRD Route to Competence: 8-Assessment and Review" (Manchester). Development Processes (Publications) Ltd.

Inner London Probation Service. (1993) "Working with Difference: A Positive and Practical Guide to Anti-Discriminatory Practice Teaching" (London) I.L.P.S.

Mehrabian, A. and Ferris, I. "Inference of attitudes from non verbal communication in two channels" The Journal of Counselling Psychology. Vol 31 (1967) p248-252

Moss, B. Marsh, J. and Stockman, S. (1997) "Disability Issues in Social Work Training and Practice". (Wrexham) Prospects Publications Ltd.

QCA (2001) The NVQ Code of Practice (London) QCA.

Rowanhill Consultants (online) "Competence: Some Practical Working Definitions." www.rowanhill.co.uk (accessed 22nd September 2005)

RSA Examinations Board. (1998) "Notes for Guidance – Vocational Qualifications". (Coventry). RSA.

University of York (2000) "Facts, Feelings and Feedback: A collaborative model for direct observation". (York) University of York

Vanheukelen. (1994) "The Evaluation of European Public Policies. European Evaluation Society Conference". Den Haag.

Wikipedia (online) "Assessment" www.enwikipedia.org/wiki/assessment (accessed 22nd September 2005)